Rites of Nature

Rites of Nature

Sabrina Krejci

STATEN HOUSE

First Edition, 2026
Published by Staten House
Printed in the United States of America

ISBN: 979-8-89860-394-6

Cover and interior design by Thistle & Thread

TABLE OF CONTENTS

You did not pick up this book to learn something new.
You picked it up because you are tired of forgetting.

We live in a world that asks us to be polished, perfect and separate from nature. But the Great Mother does not recognize the person you pretend to be in the fluorescent light. She recognizes the deep, untamed, and wild spirit that remains when the world stops watching.

Before you turn the page, take a moment to settle. Kick off your shoes, let your hair loose. Bring the part of you that has the courage to leave who you are at the tree lines, the one who is exhausted by man's calendar.

May you never walk alone, as the wild things know. They've been waiting for you to feel the drum of the land, to breathe slowly and for you to remember: you are not separate.

PART ONE

SPRING

The ice leaves in silence,
melting down the spine of a hill
where animals have already walked—
soft trails left through the dead grass.

Iris knows before anyone
she pushes through the soil,
wrapped in violet and gold—

No one teaches her, she simply
remembers the signal carried by
the lengthening light.

Even the wind shifts,
no longer carrying the
bitterness of the cold.

It feels like fingers combing
through the sleeping needles
of the ancient pines.

Great Mother,
I am thankful for your return.

You bring warmth to the land—
the soil softens, the trees stretch,
and the light grows a little stronger.

With your return, I begin again.
I plant what I hope will grow
in the Earth, in my life, and
in my spirit.

Thank you for turning the Wheel once more.

Thank you for your rhythms and
ever-changing seasons.

Help me move forward with purpose,
to tend to what matters, to listen,
and to grow.

Primrose, I see you—
as frost clings to your slender stem,
bathing in the forest's first light
of the sun spilling through the trees.

You are the first to listen,
to lean into the warmth that
has not yet arrived.

And just beneath you,
Coltsfoot begins to stir—
a golden flame rising from the
damp, dark Earth, a sun-born
secret pushing through the mud.

She comes—
the Mother, gentle in her waking stride,
each footstep striking sparks in the roots
calling the Fire to rise, and urging the Earth
to breathe again.

For days, the Robin would come each morning, singing the same song of Spring's return. Each day, the snow melted a little more and the Earth began to soften and stir. The villagers knew that Spring was on its way.

It was the Robin's song that told them this, its cheerful melody marking the end of Winter's reign. But, one morning, the Robin did not appear. The villagers grew anxious, wondering if the promise of Spring had been broken.

Had the Robin left, perhaps, to carry a new message?

On the second day, when the sky began to glow with the pink of dawn, the Robin had returned. It was perched upon the same branch, as if it had never left, and it sang its song once more.

From that day on, the Robin came without fail, and the Earth slowly began to come alive again. Flowers bloomed, buds swelled on the trees, and the warm breath of Spring spread across the land.

The Robin had not only been the first herald of Spring, but also the keeper of that promise, reminding the world that no matter how long or harsh the Winter, Spring would always return.

She left at dawn,
when the frost still clung
to the North side of the trees
and the robins had not yet
remembered their songs.

No one saw her go,
but the land felt it—
the long, low sigh of
Winter pulling back like
a tide from the shore.

They say she walked the old deer paths,
her staff in one hand,
and her cloak stitched with fallen leaves.

The rivers parted for her feet.
The moss bowed its green head.
The wind—her old companion,
wept through the heather behind her.

Up the mountain she went,
until the sky swallowed her.

We did not stop her.
Instead,
we left offerings of

bread, milk, locks of hair
at the roots of an old pine,
where she used to sit and
listen to the bones of the
world rattle.

Thank you for holding what we could not.
May the mountain remember your steps,
and when the world grows cold again,
as it always does, we will leave the
door open for your return.

The mothers would braid their daughter's hair, weaving ribbons into prayers of protection. Each strand holds memory—a story of a girl reaching womanhood, and on the peak, the old Crone has a watchful eye. She is lined with wrinkles, time etching the bridge of her nose. She smiled at the mother and daughter, seeing herself in both of them as they danced around the fire.

"No,

not a mess

not broken.

I am the wild harmony

of all who came before"

PART TWO

SUMMER

I honor you, Great Mother,
she who awakens the land,
you who stir the seeds and
swell the rivers.

You dance through the
blossoms and burn in
the Green Flame.

Thank you for your generous
wisdom, your boundless love,
and the quickening of life in
every corner of the Earth.

I see you in the tender petals
of wildflowers, in the sound of
running Water.

You are the open arms of
sunlight across green fields
bringing abundance, passion
and fertility in the sacred
union of Earth and Fire.

Let us celebrate your rising
Fire with songs and the spiral
of life.

In the summer heat,
sweat trickling down my temple,
may I be reminded of hard work,
that the one who toils will taste
the sweetness of honey.

Let the fires of the sun ignite my passion.
Let me rise with the crops growing beside
the seeds I've sown.

May I know the feeling—
primal and unbound
as you are, Great Mother.

I will tend the fields of
desire, want, and need.
Let me work towards the
harvest with blistered hands
and a full heart.

You are the salmon
spawning in rivers—
the living waters that
sustain us.

I offer my labor to the
land, and in return you
offer us life.

The Great Mother likes offerings of patchouli, ale, wine, bread, apples, and most importantly staying true to your word.

This is the truth no one speaks at the Summer Solstice feasts: When the light reaches its peak, it also begins to die. The Great Wheel turns, the days get shorter, and the shadows length-en—almost too slow to see but the wild things notice—for the animals do not keep time by the human calendar nor the clock that governs our world. They move by the deep pulse of the Earth, and the breath of light and dark.

They know what we forget: that summer is already slipping towards its end. The fox smells it in the grass, the faint sharpness under the vast green. She runs longer, hunts harder, preparing for the hunger that Winter will bring. The deer step carefully now, ears twitching between the wind, where something old stirs beneath the hill.

The bees hurry, frantic, and crowding in the clover as they swell the hive. The Queen, whose body knows the wheel is turn-ing and that honey must be stored for the harder times. Even the swallows grow restless, their wings trembling with the old memory of flight; the long southern path mapped in their blood long before they hatched.

The forest holds its breath as Meadowsweet droops in the marshy fields with its Queen's crown falling. Its sweetness turned faint and tired, along with the Tansy's yellow buttons, brown at the edges with a bitter scent thick on the wind.

Beneath the soil, in the hollow hills, the Crone stirs. The one who will wake when the green world dies. Her dreaming thickens now, she smiles in her sleep and will rise when the frost is ready.

But already her breath touches the wind and nature feels her coming. Even the Great Mother feels it, though she stands crowned in wheat with her arms full of life. She smiles, but it is a tired smile. For she too knows the secret: the seeds in her hand will not grow until they sleep, until they die, until the dark has held them.

This is the Great Turning—the unraveling of when life grows to the fullest, and so it begins to fall. When the world runs fast because the Old One will make her return.

The folk knew this once and left bread at the mound and milk at the hedge. They whispered into the standing stones as dusk thickened, asking for kindness when the Crone returned.

But for now, there's a small pulling on the loose threads, and weariness beneath the soil. Because far below, in her hollow hill, the Crone opens one pale eye and watches the world.

They say she carved the
mountains from the sorrow
in her chest.

She always lets them go,
because she must.

When the lamb falls
asleep frozen, and
the stars burn low
behind the cloud's veil,
or when the ache in your
chest has no name—

Lean on her shoulder,
maybe you will hear
the wisdom of the
Crone:

"Let go, child. Let go."

The sun paints a new canvas
of crimson, orange and gold—
all the hues Mother has gathered
through the long, bright days
of summer.

This is the harvest,
when the land turns
golden, like her hair
that spreads across the
wheat fields.

We slice her open and
witness her final child,
and as she lays there,
dying—

We lay down offerings.
We whisper thanks for
all she has given, and
all she still gives.

Great Mother,

May you know how
deeply you are loved.

How we tended to your
body with calloused hands.

May you dream of green things.
May your bones become roots.
May the silence cradle you
gently—

until the light returns.

PART THREE

AUTUMN

It's the feeling
of an Autumn day
where the dead demand
to be remembered.

Grief has a home here
but she's dressed in
flowers and love.

Because grief is all the
memories we pack into
a box and place gently
by the fire.

Let the ancestors speak,
for the Wheel has turned.

May I never forget my ancestors.
For they are the ones who paved
my path.

My ancestors were not poets, and they were no saints either. They were women who buried children, and stood up the next morning to milk the goat; men who bled into the land, cursing the sky because God would not answer but still, they believed.

When they left for America with blistered feet and hands, I was packed too. A seed in the pocket of a man who could not read, and a woman who wouldn't stop crying until the boat was pulled to shore.

They carried suitcases made of sorrow and stitched hope, crossed oceans with their Gods tucked into pockets to plant new names in the American soil. But old names do not just die, they go quiet for a while, waiting for someone to remember.

Did you miss your motherland until the day you died?
Did the snow feel the same on this side of the ocean?

The Crone came
in my dreams,
her cloak woven
from old threads.

Her breath is the
Winter wind that scours
the land clean.

"Child,
life is not soft and swift.
It flees,
but death stays—
death waits and keeps."

So, I learned patience.
I gathered the names of
things forgotten.

But I am no servant
of the grave alone.

Because where the
skulls rest,
is a foxglove—
its bells ringing
warning and wonder

in equal measure.

Deathwalking Oil

INGREDIENTS:

Aster
Benzoin
Mugwort
Poppyseed
Wormwood

For curio use only. Not for topical use or ingestion.
Keep away from children, pets, and open flame.

Death isn't the end, it is the start of something new. Enter into the liminal space and walk through the doorway. The purpose of this oil is to connect you to the energy of the ancestors.

They call me a witch, they call me wise or a madwoman in the
woods. But I am older than their names.

I drink rainwater from cupped hands, sing to the moon un-
til she turns her face, I bleed with the doe and the sowing of the
Earth. I carry the scent of death in my hair and the promise of
life in my mouth. Death may be my first teacher but life is my
ever-hungry child and behind me, in every step sprouts clover and
briar. Lamb and the shadow, cradle and the coffin, entwined like
the Old Gods meant them to be. I am She who walks between both
worlds.

Many of your kind
have forgotten me,
as they pray
to softer mothers,
gentler queens,
or gods of harvest.

But you heard the stone
crack and smelled the cold
iron of the Earth.

You felt the weight
of the frost
settle deep
in your bones.

Before the king
and before those
goddamn priests
I was the first shadow,
the blue-lipped breath
of the Old World.

I laid the hills with my hands
bared and gnarled.
I turned the rivers
to their beds with the

bones of giants.

I carved this land when
it was wild, and left no
softness in it—
nor in you.

This world rots in
its own comfort.

The same world that
fears death, endings,
and the dark.

I will make them all
learn how to kneel
through the harshness
of my Winter.

I am the end of all endings,
the Bone Mother.

and you are all mine.

Her eyes, twin amber glass,
watching the dying light—
she has watched the slowing of it.

Frost learns to etch
its own pattern into the dirt
while the sun retreats,
a pale ghost of its former self.

Her breath rises like woodsmoke
in the early hours
where dew clings to the leaves.

A slow drumbeat that signals
the end is here.

She stands between worlds—
a black body of Earth seeking the womb,
carrying the memory
of harvest into the dark.

PART FOUR

WINTER

I await the first snowflake, the silent herald of the Crone's return. I feel it in the sharp breath of the wind, in the brittleness that settles over the land.

The trees grow still beneath Her gaze, their branches naked in surrender. The air of November tastes of endings, and the truth here is laid bare. I know her footsteps draw near—ancient and inevitable, carrying a Winter storm in her palm.

I welcome you home, keeper of the cold, sculptor of stone and land. Wrap the world in your quiet dominion so that we may remember what it means to rest, to endure, and to be remade.

Across the hearth sat the Crone. She was wrapped in wool so thick it looked like a pelt. Her face was a map of a century of Winters she had survived. She didn't look up as I sat; she only nudged the copper pot deeper into the embers with a gnarled stick.

"The frost is hungry tonight," she said, her voice like grinding stones. "It's a clean kind of cruelty, the cold. It doesn't hate you. It just wants you to turn back to the Earth."

I pulled my cloak tighter, shivering as the draft found my neck. "It's brutal out there," I whispered.

"Brutal?" She let out a dry, rattling laugh. "Child, you don't know the half of it. I've seen seasons where the ground froze so deep we couldn't bury the dead until May. I've seen crops rot in the husks and mothers weeping over empty pots while the crows grew fat. Life is a silly thing—it cuts you for touching it."

"To be alive is to be a thief of time," she muttered. She finally looked at me, her eyes clouded with cataracts. "Look at you, shivering by a fire you did not build, in clothes you did not weave. You have the privilege of fear."

You see the trees
unashamed of their
skeleton and you realize
that you are more than
what life has given you.

There is dignity
in the dormancy.
A slow, deliberate
pulse underneath
the frost.

Reminding you that
nothing is ever truly lost.

So, when she asks you
to drink from cupped hands
of stillness, and makes you
look at the mirror to see
the girl who ran,
the woman who stayed,
and the ghost who is learning
how to forgive them both.

You will learn that Winter
is teaching you that
integration is alchemy.

Find a quiet place and, if you wish, light a candle.

Close your eyes. Let the warmth find you.

We are sitting at the hearthside now, all of us who have ever needed the dark to teach us something.

Listen. There is an old woman here. She has been here longer than memory. She speaks in the language of Earth and stone, of what survives the frost and what does not. Let her voice come. Let it sound like someone you recognize.

Now go further past the self you know, past the edges of who you have been. Find the version of you that has not yet arrived. She carries the wisdom you are still growing toward, the knowing that only comes with years you have not yet lived.

As you sit between the Crone who remembers, and the self who is not yet born, let what needs to be said move between them.

When you are ready, return to the fire. Return to your breath. Return to the wheel that turns, for it has always known how to find its way back.

"You want the antler,

but never fed the deer

in Winter when the snow crusted

sharp over the land.

You want the crow's eye,

but never wept beneath

the sky for the things you

could not save"

The daughters were hidden under floorboards when the men came in God's name, the women who burned in the wind.

The grandmothers boiled the afterbirth and buried it under hawthorn so the child would know protection. They screamed into the ground with their whole souls breaking, giving blood to the roots when they had hardly anything to spare, because they stayed when everything begged them to run.

Winter demands the weight of your sorrow—the part of you that is dead and will not stay still. The silence, surrender, willingness to be unmade so something older can rise. The Earth remembers, she counts every footstep. She knows what you leave behind and what you never gave.

I would rather sit alone
on a crooked tree in the
dead of Winter

with your breath in
my lungs and your
Fire in my eyes

than walk blind through
a world that has never
known the shape of
you.

In the silence of Winter's touch,
teach me the lessons of rest
and of renewal that only comes
when the world falls still.

Help me honor the pause,
to know that even in the
darkest months,
life is gathering beneath the frost.

You understand the beauty
of barren branches and
the sacredness of long nights.

Guide me through the seasons of my soul
when everything feels dormant,
and all that I have
seems lost to the cold.

She comes for the body, too,
for the soft flesh we love,
and the masks we dare not move.

Her rage is Winters rage—
a white silence so vast,
it breaks the heart open.

Her grief is endless,
like the unmarked graves
of mothers and daughters
who vanished into mist.

She carries them all—
and when she breathes,
we hear their voices in the wind.

You fear her because
she takes everything—
but without her,
there is no soil rich
enough for the seed.

No silence deep enough
for dreaming,
and no night long enough to
remember who we are.

To stand before her is to stand naked,
shivering and stripped of every excuse.

But in her hollow gaze,
know this:

that from the bones she scatters,
life will return.

The Crone's hand,
translucent as parchment,
reached trembling as she tucked a stray,
wild hair behind the Maiden's ear.

She pressed her weight into the staff
carved from ancient blackthorn.

*"Burn me well, for I have
kept the dark safe for you."*

In the turning of the Great Wheel,
mercy is a foreign tongue.
As the young Maiden looked down
and saw no stranger—
she recognized the curve of
her own jaw, and depths of her soul
in the ancient woman who
was dissolving into silver mist
between her finger tips.

This is the promise that the seasons
teach us:

*That nothing is ever truly lost,
and the end is merely the quiet gate
through which we all return.*

I honor you Ancient One.
You who carved the hills with your staff.
Who cloaked the land in stillness and snow.

Thank you for your fierce protection.
For the rest, reflection, and the deep silence
of your season.

Now your work is done.

May you retreat to stone,
to the mountain's heart,
and to dreams
through the warm months.

When the leaves turn amber and fall,
I will find you again.
I will find you in the sharp wind
through bare branches.
I will find you in the glint of frost at dawn.

Farewell, *Veiled One.*

*The Great Mother has
many names and many
faces. Who is she to you?*

www.ingramcontent.com/pod-product-compliance
Lightning Source LLC
Chambersburg PA
CBHW020654160726
47991CB00003B/1176

9 798889 860394 6